Remember the wild girl

A poetry collection about life and love for daydreamers.

Marie-Kristin Hofmann

Copyright © 2021 by Marie-Kristin Hofmann
All rights reserved.

No portion of this book may be used or reproduced without written permission from the author except for the use of brief quotation in reviews or journals.

Cover and chapter illustrations by Xuan Loc Xuan
Words by Marie-Kristin Hofmann

ISBN: 9798763919424

This is how we dreamed.
Moonlight in our mouths,
summer in our skies and
love on our lips.

For all the mind wanderers, daydreamers and
wild souls out there. There's poetry
to be found in every season.

Contents

Autumn numbness 6

Winter solitude 30

Spring awakening 51

Summer love 78

I've become quiet

with autumn, almost silent

and I don't even mourn

summer because I've forgotten

what it felt like to feel.

Personal note:

Autumn 2020. The season brings such numbness with it. I don't even remember if it's always been that way or if it's just this crazy year that makes me feel a little bit less each day.

Let me play the girl again

that waited for a boy

and look at me the way

you looked at me that day

and hold tight the love we felt,

we've lost it in the now.

Personal note:

It's so easy to lose love without even noticing. One day, you wake up and look into each other's eyes and can't find the love you once felt but if you try hard enough, you do remember. I want to go back to that time when our love was wild and each time you looked at me, I burned for you.

The autumn sky

has come too early

and the sun set

two summers too late

for me to love you

again today but I will

remember the wind

blowing through your hair

and this dream of life

I let go and how I wasn't

ready and how I'm

still not ready.

Personal note:

Letting go is hard. Letting go a love that was once so strong and that broke her wildfire heart. But the time will come when she's ready. Ready to let go and love herself a little bit more in the process.

I miss how wild
our hearts were,
how infinite we felt.
How we never saw
an end to wandering.

Personal note:

My heart aches from standing still. Being stuck in uneventfulness. It yearns for a wildness it barely remembers. But it knows it's still there. Hidden deep down and ready to break free the minute summer arrives.

I lie in the bathtub

and wait for the last

drop of water to run

out the way I ran

out of world

staring at a ceiling

full of scars

that will one day

turn into stars.

Personal note:

That day I took a bath and the autumn numbness slowly dissolved into a dim eagerness to live again. To breath autumn scents and the warm orange glow the sun leaves behind on Berlin rooftops.

Another year I'm undreaming,

not even dipping my toes

into what-ifs anymore.

Personal note:

I don't float on waves of dreams anymore. On an ocean of infinity. I don't even dip my toes into the water. I'm so tired of undreaming. I want to be hopeful again. The way I always was. I want to dream again. As big as it gets. As far as my poetry takes me.

A million stars above me,
a million souls beneath me.
I watch Berlin breathe from
my roof, the center of this city,
and wonder if I will ever
wander off again.

Personal note:

Why would I ever leave the city of lost souls? Where our wild, restless hearts flood the streets like moonlight. Where I finally found a home.

I dreamed in skies of blue
before September stole
all the light.

Personal note:

It only took a few more poems for summer to be over. The air is colder and the sun shines in a different way. And so I search for summer and long for the moments that are now passed. The ones in which I should have been a little wilder and a little braver. But maybe, just maybe, there's something even more magical to be found in autumn. Different but still beautiful.

People on trams

read books and

breathe stories they

don't share with

strangers and yet

they ache for it

in their loneliness.

Each day they

fade a bit

with autumn and

dawn, with the

cold and the

not-wandering.

Personal note:

In times like these and with the cold of October, I can almost touch the loneliness every time I ride the tram. It speaks to me like the city does. With each day not moving, I barely remember the wanderlust I once had. The excitement each new journey and new place held. How wild and alive I felt. I want that rush again.

I spill wine glass rainbows

on crinkled pages.

My life is a prologue

to next summer.

Personal note:

When will I be loved? Cheers to white wine on rooftops and long solitary nights with stacks of books in my lap. Until it's the final night of senseless waiting and hoping and a simple enjoying of the pure extasy of being me.

We used to dream

our heads stuck solid

on wings of words

unspoken and wisps of worlds

unlived because we were

a little too scared and

a little too apathetic to break

the unsettling silence of

settling for nothingness.

Personal note:

I don't want to search for safety in numbness. I don't want to live in a forever summerless world. I need to dream again.

October is a polaroid

dusty with summer dreams

and could-have-beens.

Personal note:

The season of nostalgy. But why does it have to be just that? How about we live this autumn like it's the summer we've been waiting for?

I still see

summer stars

shimmer on your

summer skin

where autumn

now sits in that

empty space of

a lost you.

Personal note:

I still feel the memories of summer in your love. When you were happy and hopeful. When your kiss held that little promise of excitement and you weren't autumn-numb.

Is this my tomorrow?

A morning sun

spilled into a someone

that never was

and never would be.

A daydream

drifting into a dead end

that always was

and always would be.

Personal note:

Your life doesn't have to be a dead end or a daydream. Why do we always stay behind our beyond?

How did our wildfire hearts

turn to November dust

in our hollowed-out hands?

Personal note:

I can't stop mourning how quickly summer passed this year. And how autumn is a reminder of all the lives we didn't live and all the adventures we didn't have.

Take me back to when my

heart was gold and

home was everywhere.

Personal note:

Take me back to that time I was wild. When home was everywhere. In hopeful beginnings and goodbyes. In soft openings and night sky dances.

Let me live in the
suspension of life
as everyone lives it.
Let me float just a
little while longer on
no things of matter.
Let me drift on the
not going anywhere.

Personal note:

Adulting is hard. And why are our lives so predetermined? Do we have to copy each other's paths? Follow them in straight lines and die a little bit inside? Is living really supposed to feel that way?

I see ghosts

of summer sunsets

in the November sky

and dream of you.

Personal note:

I dream of summer and you. When we were both a little wilder and a little more in love.

Street light trees bare
to the branch glow
neon gold like fake
summer love in this
late autumn madness.

Personal note:

Last autumn was weird and sad and restless. Like a fake promise of cosy nights spent in old cafés and hopeful walks and dreams of summer wildness. It's not even melancholy I feel anymore. It's hopelessness and disillusion.

The infinite sky

an ocean of clouds

a whisper of sunset dreams

now a grey nothingness

of an empty year and an

even emptier heart.

Personal note:

I miss falling in love with the grandness of it all. The world. The wild. Life. Love. The little things.

Solitude is drip drop
drizzling out of
clouds so brim
with poetry rain.

Personal note:

There's poetry to be found in solitude. Even if the sky is grey.
Even if it seems like the world won't stop raining. Rilke knew
that already.

I was made for the rain.

For rain on the road,

the never-ending road.

And it rains and rains and rains

while I roam and roam and run

inside a rain-soaked

rain-roaming kind of world

homeless and cold.

Personal note:

For all the restless souls out there. Who roam the world, who can't stop running, who are constantly on the move. Maybe, we were made for this. For the rain. For getting lost. For not finding a home. But maybe, the whole world is our home already. And maybe, one day, we'll be our own home instead.

The polaroid sun
in her palm dusty
with memories rises
without a trace of
the two people who
once loved each other.

Personal note:

All she had left of him was a polaroid. And a heart filled with nostalgy. Of a summer love and a sunrise that meant the world to her. That changed her life. So, she smiled, forever remembering the magic.

Winter solitude

And all the lives
we never lived
dissolve into
December dust.

Another year we didn't dream.

Personal note:

Let's not give up on dreaming big. Those unlived years serve as a reminder to live the way we want to live. To make use of every day. To not have our dreams become like dusty old books we slowly forget about it.

It's January, it's cold and
I search the sky for summer
like I always do.

Personal note:

Some things don't change. The way I still mourn summer memories and wish for the cold and darkness to fade faster than they do. Give me that blue sky life back, please.

I turn skyward where

vapor trails aren't

white roads or clean

slates for a new

home but distance

that doesn't stop

spreading.

Do you hear the paper

birds sing? I'm still

a winter silence

going nowhere.

Personal note:

The sky is the limit and I wish it wasn't. There was a time when it wasn't. When you could hop on a plane and never stop leaving. Where there was home in goodbyes and new beginnings.

Outside the window
the day is ending and I still
watch the snow fall on my
morning reflection.

Personal note:

Winter makes me even more contemplative. I could do nothing all day but watch the snow fall and turn the outside world into the color of solitude while I watch and wait and that's all I do.

Berlin sunsets seep
through my window
like the world was
still wild and winter
was just a myth
we told each other
and life was not
on hold.

Personal note:

Even the beauty of a Berlin sunset seems pointless this winter
and I hope to find meaning in summer again.

Lemonade hearts

lavender love

lips longing

for anything

but loneliness.

Personal note:

How much do we crave human connection now. Just a touch of hearts, a touch of lips. A touch of summer to wash away the loneliness that tears at us.

I can't keep waiting for words
that will never come
out of your mouth the way
I daydreamed them.

Personal note:

We hope for those words and the love that we dreamed up, but it doesn't come. Because we can't always depend on someone else giving us the love we should give ourselves first. And we can't wait for half a love because we've always needed more.

I should have seen

the goodbye in your eyes

from the start.

Personal note:

Your eyes screamed goodbye. Your heart did. But I was deaf to it all because I was in love. Because my heart was hopeful and yours wasn't. Because I wasn't afraid to love but you were. You left and I didn't look back.

The way he lies there
his bones stone cold
staring at me like I'm
the abyss of loneliness,
still, reaching for me with
his hand not his heart only
to pull back right before the
final touch out of his fear
of tenderness because what if
he did feel something, even just
a tremor of softheartedness.
There would be too much
warmth and going back from
warmth to coldness
hurts.

Personal note:

We all know the fear of opening up. So, we remain cold to protect ourselves. Warmth is beautiful. It feels so much better than the cold. But when you lose it, it drains your heart to the point of a pain so deep, emptiness becomes the safer choice.

Somewhere behind the moon

you'll find her

lost in night thoughts.

Personal note:

Crescent moon shadows grow beneath her eyelids into trees of dreams. You knew, she'd never be your sun, but she'd always make you think.

Through the quiet

of the night

and the magic

of words

I enter worlds

of someone else's

imagination.

Personal note:

I love staying up all night reading. Getting lost in other worlds and the coziness of a good book.

She was a windowsill

type of girl

quietly dreaming

about the world

from afar.

Personal note:

She was a daydreamer. A mind wanderer. But sometimes, she got so lost in watching, in dreaming that she forgot to actually live. So spread your wings, girl. Be wild. Get off that windowsill and live a little.

She loves her

lonely moments,

the silence away

from the crowds,

when it's just her

daydreaming.

Personal note:

For all the introverts who gain their energy from being alone. Who need their quiet moments, too. With their nose in a book and their head in the clouds.

Rosy cheeks suddenly remember

a sun-kissed romance

long forgotten.

Personal note:

Sometimes we forget. We forget what it felt like to be in love. How we stood in the pouring summer rain and really knew what it meant to live. To love. To laugh. Sometimes though, we do remember. Something comes up that triggers a long-forgotten memory.

There's a feeling for leaving

in the February sun

the way it sings of restless souls

waiting for the snow

to melt into summer seas

just worlds away.

Personal note:

I need to break free. I need to leave. Not indefinitely, just wander a little. Travel a little. Get lost a little. It's been more than a year of this madness. A year of restlessness unlived. A year of wildness to be tamed. A year of almost going numb. Let me float on summer seas. Just let me live a little.

Where are the sunsets

in your eyes?

The wild dreams

and summer smiles?

Personal note:

Sometimes I'm disillusioned by life. I have all these romantic hopes and dreams. I want to be wild and free. I want to love and dance and laugh. I want to feel the intensity of it all but sometimes it feels like life can't be more than a bad movie. Never as wild as I'd dreamed it to be, never as adventurous.

On Valentine's Day,

for the first time in weeks

the winter sun was out

but she didn't dance.

Her wilted wallflower eyes

searched for spring in

old goodbyes.

Personal note:

The February sky turned black and another heart dissolved into nostalgy. How could I ever bring her back?

It was winter all summer.
The sun wasn't gold but
yellowed like worn-out
cocktail dresses and I bathed
in the memory of seaside skins
and love songs and light that had
left me and the world and so a
life lived not even in halves
but quarters was the
new normal.

Personal note:

The new normal. A phrase we have heard so many times and got so acquainted with. But did it have to be lost time? A life lived not even in halves? Or could it be a chance for something else? A time of introspection?

I float on

bathtub thoughts

searching deep

down within

for a heart

I've somehow

lost.

Personal note:

She lay in the bathtub, naked in the naked night and her spine grew slowly into a tree of moonlight flowers sharing in her solitude.

At the edge of a year unlived
I found my dreams again
and this time, I'm not
letting them go.

Personal note:

I can't believe I didn't dream for a whole year. Forgot what living meant. Really living. I need to wake up.

I remembered the wild girl

every time I saw her soul

in the neon pastel sky.

Personal note:

Another Berlin summer story: She was wild and lost and restless. She was as much pastel colored clouds as she was neon light sunsets.

She sat there
a wild heart on a chair
with gin lips and
nightlife eyes.

The Gatsby Girl.

Longing for more
in the shallowness
of it all.

Personal note:

For everyone out there who dreams big. Who wants more than a shallow conversation. More than a simple life. And a half-hearted love. Who wants to live and love and cry and laugh. Even in times like these. I wrote this poem during my first Berlin nightlife encounters when Corona didn't exist yet. Longing for times like these now.

With each daydream

she weaved

her pastel heart

into the sky.

Personal note:

Her heart floats on pastel clouds, all the way up into the daydreamers' sky. She watches the normal people down below as they go by their daily business, each one of them becoming more and more dreamless as the days pass them by. To pink sky nights and rooftop dreams. To wild hearts and Berlin souls.

There's a beyond in each sunset.

Where the world doesn't end.

Where time isn't wasted.

Where life doesn't

walk away.

Personal note:

I try to watch every sunset I can get on my Berlin rooftop. Each one is different and each one holds an afterglow. I sit there and imagine that it reaches past the earth, past the end of the world as we imagine it. Into a beyond that we can't even dream up. Into all the lives we never lived but should.

"Why can't the world be pastel colored?"
She asked.
He replied:
"Because life is better lived intensely."

Personal note:

A pastel colored, white tea world would be a lovely world. A peaceful world. But it would lack the more vivid colors. It would lack the intensity that life requires. It would lack the wildness.

Her eyes were

the color of daydreams,

each shade a different

kind of could-be.

Personal note:

Are you one of the daydreamers, too? Your head stuck in the clouds, always somewhere else than in the here and now. Somewhere drifting skyward with your thoughts. And isn't that beautiful? To dream up worlds. And wouldn't it be even more beautiful to really live them?

And my wild little heart
hurts from dreaming less.

Personal note:

I miss dreaming big. I miss a world without borders, I miss the feeling of limitlessness. I miss the excitement of getting lost and ending up where the wind takes me. Where my wild little heart dreams of going next.

The people I meet

blur into an undiscernible mass.

None of them are meaningful

unlike the places that merge

into my scattered mess

of a vagabond's heart.

Personal note:

The road is where I belong. An endless wanderer, on the search for a home. Home is a feeling I only find when I travel. Home is leaving and never arriving.

She had a wanderer's eyes
always sparkling
with that sense of
somewhere else.

Personal note:

Once a traveler, always a traveler. Even if this year kept us all from wandering, our hearts remained as wild as ever. And the day will come when we can all be wanderers again.

I saw something sparkle

in her eyes that day.

The urge to move. To leave.

To never stay.

Personal note:

Do you know this restlessness? The urge to move, to wander, to never settle because there's still so much to see and explore. And that urge is even stronger in times of Corona because it was made impossible for a while. Can you relate?

Loving her was a

journey into neverland.

It opened up a world

I had only known

from my daydreams.

Personal note:

She was a daydreamer and mind wanderer. She dreamed up worlds beyond anything he could imagine. She dreamed big. And that's why he fell for her.

She had a spring
silence mouth and
white tea eyes that
watched the wild
world be without a
single word of
shallowness.

Personal note:

There's a certain beauty to a quiet spring day. We need to listen to that beauty. We need to watch the world just be. Without taking from it with our shallow words.

The way the willow

gently danced above

her head and the afternoon

breeze carried with it a late

May kind of solitude.

Personal note:

I love these late May kind of afternoons, the warm breeze rustling through the pages of my poetry book, with my heart so full of solitude and a pure appreciation for nature.

I trace dots of sunlight
along pages of poetry
white and soft as
swan feathers.
Oh, the beauty of
spring solitude!
And yet my heart
beats for summer
more than ever.

Personal note:

I love introspection. Quietly reading a book or reading between the clouds. But I also daydream about summer nights around campfires, about real and deep connections. Maybe we always want what we can't have instead of appreciating the here and now as it is and the opportunities it provides.

She was the type of girl that
searched for daisies in
sidewalk cracks.

Personal note:

A hundred summers won't compare to the summer that shone from her heart. She exuded hope and life and love for the little things.

Unspoken questions
tumble from your eyes
into your mouth and
with each touch of lips
I understand a little bit
more about you and
the bigger picture.

Personal note:

Eyes can speak so much louder than words sometimes. And sometimes, we feel more than all the words we hear. There's poetry in a kiss. Because with each touch of lips, you grasp a little bit more of who the other person is and what their heart has to tell you. What questions move their soul. What bigger picture there is to them.

The shadows of spring

on my wall and

thoughts of you like

pressed flowers in

poetry books.

Personal note:

Your intrinsically woven into my summer memories. Like a pressed flower in my poetry book, you remain. A thought that lingers. A love that stays. Quietly.

Red wine spills

philosophy from your lips

and I watch it burn a

home into my heart

with each shared sip of

holding back a little less.

Personal note:

Red wine conversations go deeper than white wine ones. And so, this spring, with you, days blur into one and conversations become poetry.

Meet me in that poppy field

where spring is in the breeze

and summer in the sky

and you are not

a daydream.

Personal note:

You told me I was like a poppy field to you, with a slight spring breeze blowing. I loved the comparison and I still do. You're my summer sky. In your arms, it's always June. I'm so happy to have you and so glad, you are not a daydream.

I either want a love like poetry
or no love at all.

Personal note:

Either love me like poetry, or don't love me at all. I want a love like the love us poets write about. A love as romantic as sunset tears. As poetic as forest meadows. As wild as ocean waves.

We lived in paper

bird skies folding

our what-ifs

into origami hearts.

Personal note:

We were almost lovers. So wildly in love and yet so afraid of it. And so we never moved past our what-ifs. We folded our words into paper birds and sent them to the sky. But they remained unspoken. Forever sealed in our two origami hearts that just couldn't take the risk.

Don't fall for someone
that doesn't have
a spark of wild
in their eyes.

Personal note:

Fall for someone who makes you live a little bit more. Laugh a little bit more and love a little bit more. Who wants more from life just as much as you do. Who makes it all one big adventure.

Every drop of her gin
held a lost world of
night sky dances.

Personal note:

I miss the excitement and the rush of nightlife. Not the hordes of people or the unnecessary small talk, not the shallowness. But the intensity of it all. The dancing and laughing and the search for a deeper meaning in the mess of it all.

I live in the imaginary wild

and it's as soft

as summer.

Personal note:

I daydream until the imaginary wild blends into the real world. Into the life I was used to. The life of the lost ones. The restless souls. The wild wanderers. Forward to summer.

And with the universe

being so infinite

why shouldn't

we dream a little?

Personal note:

Let's not give up on all the dreams we once had. We tend to forget about them and time passes us by so much faster than we think.

There is a soft whisper of hope
somewhere down the road
to rewilding.

Personal note:

Dance with me above the rooftops of a restless city. Kiss me until we're both soaked in poetry rain. Of a summer night that will never end unless we stop dreaming. Let's rewild.

This is how

we dreamed.

Moonlight

in our mouths,

summer

in our skies

and love

on our lips.

Personal note:

We never stopped dreaming. We saw magic in the moon and in starlit nights. Each day was summer. Each heart we met, we loved. What a beautiful daydream it all was. And so why shouldn't we also live it?

We counted

ocean waves

and clouds in

cloudless skies

and summer

trailed behind us

like our youth

wasn't half gone.

Personal note:

Each summer is a chance to pretend we're still young and life is spread out in front of us and we can do anything we dream of.

There was gold

entangled in her hair

like a song of summer

as she watched

the sun set in

his balcony eyes.

Personal note:

There's poetry in the way we slowly fall in love with someone and suddenly realize it when we look at them and know.

In June,

our hearts were pure

and light and full of summer.

Because we didn't know yet

how afraid we were

to love each other.

Personal note:

There's such a lightness that comes with summer and summer romances. But they have another thing in common. They end as quickly as they started. And many times because we're all a little bit too afraid of loving.

We fell in love

because we were both

sunset souls.

Personal note:

We were both romantic in the way we longed for something more in each sunset. We saw a magic in it others didn't see. We dreamed about a world beyond our world.

When July came,

her heart started

blooming and the words

sprung from it

like wildflowers.

Personal note:

For some reason, we're happier in summer. We appreciate life more than we do in any of the other seasons. We notice more of the beauty of it all. How the wildflowers bloom. And our hearts open up for July poetry.

I lost something

a thousand sunsets ago

and found it again

in your summer sky eyes.

Personal note:

Sometimes we lose a piece of ourselves. We lose a little bit of our zest for life. And sometimes, we meet someone who brings it all back. Who brings us back to our old selves, who settles us back inside of our love for life.

He kissed the silence

from her lips and

spread it past the night

and in his smile

she settled and found

a world of warmth

and in his hand a home.

Personal note:

She didn't say anything. She didn't find the courage to. And with him, she didn't need to. He kissed the words from her lips and knew.

You were like that warm
orange glow dripping from
the early summer sky.
A home painted in
evening sun rays.

Personal note:

Everything you said and did exuded warmth. Every touch a soft sun ray, every kiss and every word. I never found a home in a place, but I found a home in you.

Girl from the clouds

with those poetry eyes

I dream of you

sometimes.

Boy from the ocean

with those seafarer eyes

I think of you

sometimes.

Personal note:

A boy from the ocean met a girl from the clouds. There was poetry in their love. In the way they touched. The way they talked. The way they became one.

The way we sat there
opposite each other
on that rooftop
soaked in rain like
we could become art.

Personal note:

That summer we spent almost entirely on the roof, watching the lights come up and all those lost Berlin souls, us among them, roam the streets. And we felt infinite. Powerful. We were happy then.

We were half a summer love

but a forever kind of memory.

Personal note:

It doesn't always matter how long a love lasts. Sometimes, it's about the intensity. And there's not many loves as intense as a summer romance. There's a certain magic to it. It changed my heart forever.

You and I,

we are cloud swimmers.

We bath in could-bes

and what-ifs,

in eternal summer

and imaginary love.

Personal note:

We are cloud swimmers. We get high on daydreaming and mid-air floating.

We were both wanderers,
restlessness dripping from
our wild lips like rain
and even if no place would
ever truly be home for us,
I found it in the way you
held my hand that day.

Personal note:

If the world doesn't hold a home for us, if we're a little bit lost and don't really know where we belong. Even if we stay eternal wanderers, we can still find a home in another person. Maybe even a better one.

We talked about

sunsets and leaving,

love and being lost,

heartbreak and hope.

It was one of those

rare moments when

a stranger became magic.

Personal note:

And just like that a 2am conversation turned into magic and a stranger became her universe. Isn't it funny how we sometimes have these instant connections with people we meet for the first time? And how we open up to them at night? After some wine under a starlit sky.

Her heart lived

at the edge of the world

where goodbyes faded

into nothingness and

eternal summer

ruled the road.

Personal note:

For all the wanderers out there. Who never stop leaving. Who lose and find themselves at the same time. Who go anywhere and nowhere.

I was at the sea again,

two years and

six hundred sunsets

had passed and it all

came back to me.

Life was still right there

in front of me.

And a pandemic and foolish boys
were never really standing in my way.

Personal note:

There I was, at the sea again after an eternity of not-wandering. And I felt alive again for a moment. I remembered a distant feeling. The urge to break free. The urge to leave for good. To unnumb and rewild.

I wish you and I,

we were more

than just a summer.

Personal note:

He was a hope that died with the last day of summer. And maybe it was exactly meant to be that way. A wild memory, a summer romance that never fully fades from the heart forever keeping it alive.

As July ended and

I let you go

there was half a summer

left for me.

Personal note:

And sometimes, we have to let go. Of a love or another heart. And it's hard. It might be the hardest thing to do. But it can ultimately free you, too. And finally open you up to your own self.

"Where did summer go?"
She asked the lavender clouds
as July turned to sunset dust.

Personal note:

In the beginning of summer, we're always drunk on this grand hope that this time our lives will finally change forever. Until they don't. We always live for the summer until we don't live it at all.

Can you feel the end of summer?

The way our hearts long for aliveness
like it was still June but it's August
and now there's nothing more than
regrets and silent dreams of a
life that we never fully live.
Not even next summer.

Personal note:

With the end of summer approaching, we reflect on all the lives we never lived and all the things we never did and how regretting something sucks.

Another summer leaves

the city through the tram

window and flickers orange,

a last goodbye to light

in strangers' eyes.

Personal note:

On one of those last August days, I sat on the tram and watched summer leave in a sunset reflection.

There's an afterglow

of summer in the way

her eyes still sparkle

and the sunlight fades

from his skin into

a new tomorrow.

Personal note:

There's summer in the way their love is light and simple. The way she looks at him and knows. The way her eyes sparkle when he tells her that she's beautiful. The way the sun sets but they linger.

Printed in Great Britain
by Amazon